Original title:
Life's Meaning: Still Pending

Copyright © 2025 Creative Arts Management OÜ
All rights reserved.

Author: Hugo Fitzgerald
ISBN HARDBACK: 978-1-80566-070-5
ISBN PAPERBACK: 978-1-80566-365-2

The Quiet Before Clarity

In the morning, I sip my tea,
Wondering who I'll pretend to be.
Should I dance or just sit still?
Decisions pile up like a big hill.

A sock without its pair, oh dear,
Is this chaos or just cheer?
Am I lost or have I found?
With riddles swirling all around.

The cat just stared, judging me so,
As I juggled dreams like a circus show.
Maybe I'll rise, or take a nap,
In this weird, captivating trap.

So laugh away the ticking clock,
With every tick, I gain a block.
I'll find clarity with a kid's riddle,
Or perhaps just an awful fiddle.

The Dawn of What Could Be

Morning breaks with a wink,
Coffee spills, don't you think?
Dreams are vague, like fog on glass,
Hopes get stuck in the hourglass.

To-do lists float like balloons,
Chasing goals but meeting tunes.
The toast burns, oh what a feat,
Yet we laugh, can't take a seat.

Shadows of a Fading Whisper

Life's a joke without a punch,
We laugh and dance, it's all a bunch.
Echoes fade, like sound on air,
We search for truth in the fair's despair.

Glimpses tease, we chase the tail,
A weird parade in the twilight pale.
Questions linger like last night's fries,
Yet we keep cracking, rolling our eyes.

In Pursuit of the Unseen

Chasing dreams in an old shoe,
Can't catch the breath, not even a clue.
The map's upside down, oh what a sight,
We wander along, in the fading light.

Reality jingles a quirky tune,
While we juggle worries beneath the moon.
Barbecue sauce stains all our shirts,
Still, we embrace, and ignore the quirks.

Questions Beneath the Surface

Underneath the laughter's mask,
We seek the answers, a daunting task.
Why's the sun so far away?
It laughs at us when we go astray.

We dive deep in a kiddie pool,
Searching for wisdom, what a fool.
Yet we float, enjoying the ride,
Questions bubble, but smiles abide.

Flickers of Hope Amidst the Fog

In a world of coffee spills,
Dreams sometimes miss their drills.
A cat sits plotting all night,
While I chase thoughts out of sight.

The toaster burns my toast again,
I laugh and count it as a win.
Who knew the bread had such flair?
Yet here I am, without a care.

Puzzles in the Twilight

A thousand pieces on the floor,
Not sure what I'm searching for.
The cat steals one and runs away,
Fluffy thief, what do you say?

In the evening glow I muse,
Is it chocolate or just a ruse?
A riddle wrapped in a snack,
If found, there's no turning back.

The Veil of Untold Stories

Beneath the blankets of my doubts,
Are tales of shoes and mismatched socks.
I ponder whims of flying ducks,
And laugh at plans that just suck.

With every sneeze, a plot unfolds,
Of adventures that never get told.
Are there fairies in my old shoes?
Maybe it's just my poor excuse.

A Tapestry of Unfinished Thoughts

I wove a dream with twinkling lights,
Then fell asleep on cozy nights.
The tapestry has bits of flair,
Yet dizziness leads to despair.

In threads of laughter, I get stuck,
Stitching plans with a touch of luck.
When morning comes, I start anew,
With hopeful threads of bolder hue.

Merely a Mirage

A rabbit in a top hat, oh what a sight,
Pulling dreams from the air, with a flick and a bite.
Chasing shadows of purpose, in a whimsical game,
Finding joy in the chaos, nothing's ever the same.

Socks without partners, they frolic and dance,
In a world of mismatched, they take every chance.
A jester's sweet laughter, he stumbles and trips,
The meaning of nonsense, in wild ocean sips.

Unsung Stories

The snail with a suitcase, so slow on his way,
Dreams of far lands, just a leaf for his stay.
Whispers of possums discussing their fate,
Each night they debate on a plate full of bait.

A dandelion's wish, gets blown to the breeze,
It dreams of a kingdom, all covered in cheese.
Yet in a puddle, it finds its own cheer,
Splashing with laughter, as it floats year to year.

Interludes of Reflection

In an empty balloon, thoughts start to swirl,
Colorful notions dart and twirl.
A hedgehog with shades, sipping sweet tea,
Contemplates sharply, what it means to be free.

Tickles from time, in a land full of jest,
The crickets hum softly, while they take a rest.
A sock puppet's wisdom, so quirky and loud,
Reminds us to laugh, be silly, be proud.

Quantum Whispers

A cat in a spaceship, exploring the skies,
A tale of confusion, yet gleams in his eyes.
Parallel worlds where the peanut is king,
Winning old battles, just pies and cheese strings.

The toaster's advice on the bread of the day,
"Don't take it too seriously, just let it play."
With giggles and chuckles, the universe spins,
In the quirkiest corners, our journey begins.

Threads of Uncertainty

In a world of wobbly string,
I wonder what tomorrow may bring.
The sock seems lost, the cat's on a spree,
Was that my last slice of pizza? Oh me!

Thought I had plans, then they went poof,
Like my old goldfish, off to the roof.
Sometimes I dance with a twist of fate,
Oh well, at least I'm never late.

Wrap me in questions, like a burrito tight,
Salsa on the side, serve it up right.
The universe chuckles, it's all just a game,
A board made of jelly and a piece just the same.

So here's to tomorrow, and maybe the next,
With a hopeful heart and a mind quite perplexed.
I'll spin on this merry-go-round of confusion,
Laughing at riddles in curious fusion.

When the Stars Forget to Shine

When stars in the sky decide to nap,
I'll throw a party, set a grand trap.
Candles can flicker, but they won't replace,
The glittering sparkle of a star's embrace.

I'll fill up my cup with stardust and glee,
A cosmic mixology, just for me!
With hiccups of laughter, we'll dance on the floor,
Even if Orion has stepped out the door.

Galaxies giggling, hiding behind clouds,
I'm still here, bright and talking too loud.
A comet's a-chasing, but what's the big deal?
Let's find the lost stars; let's make it a reel!

So even in darkness, let's throw out our dreams,
On a trampoline of laughter, we'll bounce through the beams.
And if it gets trippy, well, that's just our fate,
Who knew that forgetting would feel so great?

In Search of the Light

With a flashlight flickering, I'm off to explore,
Searching for wisdom behind the next door.
Is that a shadow, or my laundry pile high?
Why do my socks always vanish? Oh my!

I'm trekking through thoughts, with snacks in my pack,
A journey of questions stacked up on my back.
Is the answer out there in a peanut butter jar?
Or am I just dreaming, wishing on a star?

With a trail mix of worries and giggles galore,
Every step taken reveals something more.
I'll seek out the sunrise, ride waves of delight,
While dodging the moments that leave me in fright.

And if I trip over, oh what a fine mess,
I'll laugh as I tumble, it's all just a test.
In search of the light, I remember this rhyme:
The adventure is sweeter when taken in time.

Labyrinth of Longing

In a maze made of wishes, I wander around,
Hoping I'll find that lost frisbee I found.
I chase my own tail, like a curious pup,
Wondering if there's a sign-up for "Fill Up!"

Each corner I turn brings a new kind of flair,
Is that ice cream I smell, or a lost teddy bear?
With a map drawn in crayon, I'm ready to roam,
Maybe I'll find treasure, or just a new home.

Bumps on the path, like life's little quirks,
I trip on my hopes, then go back to work.
Navigating the turns with a chuckle and cheer,
What's just a pitfall can lead to a beer.

So here's to the winding, the twists, and the bends,
Embrace the absurd, let the laughter extend.
In the labyrinth's heart, with a heart that time's frayed,
I'll find my own way, and I won't be dismayed.

Whispers of Tomorrow

In a world with a plan, yet no map,
We dance like ducks in a grand mishap.
With coffee cups held like magic wands,
Dreaming of strolling through faraway lands.

The clock ticks loud, do we hear the beat?
Chasing our tails on a disco street,
We giggle at thoughts that jump and play,
Searching for meaning in a foam ballet.

The Unwritten Journey

With a suitcase of hopes and socks unpaired,
We trek on paths that seem quite scared.
Map quest converted into a jigsaw,
Who knew all those landmarks were just a flaw?

We laugh at the signs with arrows askew,
Risking it all on a whim or two.
With a few nuts and bolts of curious cheer,
We leap into chaos, it's always near.

Chasing Shadows of Purpose

Running in circles, a merry-go-round,
Purpose plays peekaboo, never found.
Like a cat with a laser that sparks delight,
We're all just chasing, day and night.

In the land of the lost and the oddly bizarre,
We ponder our fate like a fallen star.
And while we tumble through every riddle,
Life tickles our toes and plays the fiddle.

Echoes of a Questioned Existence

In a circus of thoughts, juggling dreams,
We search for potholes in life's wild streams.
With popcorn and laughter, we sit on a log,
Trying to decode life's twittering dog.

Like a squirrel with acorns, we scurry about,
On this maze of what it's all about.
When the lights turn low, we giggle and sigh,
Is this the grand show, or just a pie in the sky?

The Edge of Understanding

I searched for wisdom in a shoe,
But all I found was just one glue.
The answers danced like socks in air,
While I just laughed and lost my hair.

I asked a cat for sage advice,
It stared at me, not once too nice.
I guess it felt I'd lost my grip,
As I explained my life's little trip.

The trees just chuckled, swaying free,
Whispering secrets, not to me.
I tried to join their leafy chat,
But all they spoke was, "Don't be fat!"

Each day I greet the world with cheer,
While sipping coffee, never fear.
The quest for sense can be a joke,
So grab some laughs, and just provoke!

Searching for the Unfamiliar

I looked for truths in strange old shoes,
Hoping they'd share their ancient views.
But all they offered was some dust,
And a small worm that I could trust.

I ventured deep into the wood,
To find what's strange, as best I could.
What did I find? A squirrel in specs,
Counting acorns, no time for hexes.

The mountains laughed at my bold quest,
Said wisdom thrives in silly jest.
And as I stumbled, tripped and fell,
A fairy asked, "Are you unwell?"

With jokes that soared like kites in flight,
I pondered silly thoughts at night.
The unknown's charm is often missed,
In simple joys, we do persist!

Conversations with the Infinite

I tried to chat with the great vast sky,
But all it gave me was a fly.
I swatted hard, but it came back,
The universe laughs at my lack!

I pondered deep on cosmic themes,
What if it's all just silly dreams?
The stars just winked with puns galore,
Encouraging laughter, never a bore.

The planets spun in perfect tune,
While I yelled questions to the moon.
It chuckled low, replied with glee,
"Stop thinking hard, just dance with me!"

My deep thoughts drifted into space,
With humor wrapped in cosmic grace.
The infinite found a funny mood,
In laughter's glow, I understood!

A Stillness of Wonder

I sat in silence, what to find?
A moment's grace to ease my mind.
But all I spied was Mr. Frog,
Leaping high on a half-baked log.

He croaked at me with joyful mirth,
As if he'd uncovered life's true worth.
Before I knew, I joined his song,
In this odd duet, I felt so wrong.

The flowers giggled, petals shook,
Whispered secrets, quiet as a book.
With every bloom that dared to peek,
I laughed at things I couldn't speak.

In stillness, wonder felt so light,
As life became a silly flight.
Chasing whims in a world so grand,
Searching for joy, hand in hand!

Whims of the Open Road

The highways stretch, a winding joke,
As I chase after clouds that poke.
Every bend holds a silly twist,
In this trip, who could resist?

With a map turned upside down,
I laugh while searching for that town.
My GPS likes to play coy,
It's a travel game, oh what joy!

Bumper stickers dance in the breeze,
Silly phrases put me at ease.
From coffee spills to missing socks,
Every mile's a box of paradox.

So here I zoom, with my quirks and glee,
The open road's where I find me.
Chasing sunsets, I steer and sing,
Oh, the fun that the unknown can bring!

The Art of Waiting

In lines that twist like spaghetti,
I ponder why I'm feeling petty.
The clock ticks slow, a stubborn tease,
While I count the dust on my knees.

Every second a tiny dance,
I wonder if I missed my chance.
A texting duel with my own thumb,
Oh look, there's a pigeon, how fun!

The barista's skills, a coffee delight,
But here I am, waiting with fright.
With every sip, I tell myself,
This art of waiting's on a shelf!

Anxiety jolts, but that's just me,
Laughing at how chaotic life can be.
So I embrace this strange ballet,
Waiting can be a funny play!

Where Silence Speaks

In quiet corners, thoughts collide,
Where whispers hide, and laughs abide.
I sip my tea, and there it flows,
A giggle blooms, and silence grows.

Every pause, a chance to jest,
In solitude, I'm at my best.
The silence seems to have a grin,
A chuckle shared with where I've been.

Mundane moments, you silly muse,
You've snatched my boredom; I've got the blues.
In silence bright, I find my cheer,
Where quiet rooms are fun to steer.

So here I sit, away from the clamor,
With silence casting its unwritten glamour.
Finding laughter in a thought or two,
In tranquil stillness, I laugh anew!

A Journey in Solitude

With my shadow as my trusty side,
We embark on this solo ride.
Talking to trees, oh what a sight,
They nod along, feeling quite bright.

Stumbling over roots, I laugh in jest,
Nature's way of putting me to test.
Each fallen leaf whispers a tune,
In the great outdoors, I'm a buffoon.

The sun leads with a playful glow,
While clouds gather for a surprise show.
I dance on paths where no one goes,
Creating stories in nature's prose.

So here I roam in solitude's grace,
With chuckles bouncing in this vast space.
Every step, a giggle on the trail,
In my journey alone, I shall not fail!

Unfolding the Infinite

In a world of endless chatter,
We chase dreams, making them fatter.
Why do we strive? What's the score?
Ask the cat, who just wants a door.

Coffee cups filled with worry,
But the dish runs away in a hurry.
Yet, we laugh and dance through the fray,
A chocolate cake at the end of the day.

Maps covered in crumbs, jigsaw alert,
Puzzles of joy, and stress in our shirt.
Are we lost? Not quite, I dare,
Just making footprints in cosmic air.

So let's juggle our plans and our dreams,
Like clowns with oversized ice cream.
Life's a circus, and oh what a scene,
We're all just actors in a wobbly routine.

Notes from a Journey

On the road with no GPS guide,
Just a sandwich and a bear inside.
Why seek answers, with snacks in hand?
Each bite tastes better than a master plan.

Our suitcase is packed with laughter,
Got foraging tips—what's the matter?
Socks mismatched, blissfully bright,
Who needs style when you're feeling right?

Maps crumpled, adventures unsold,
Wind in our hair, and stories unfold.
Some days we dance, some days we trip,
But oh what a journey, on this wibbly ship!

So here's to the roads we meander,
To snacks and giggles, and good old banter.
Whatever awaits, we'll shout, "Hooray!"
For each mile we take, is a fun cabaret.

Reflections in the Mist

In a haze where thoughts play hide and seek,
The mirror's cracked, my ankle's weak.
I ponder the deep, the wise, the grand,
Only to find I've lost my lunch band.

With foggy glasses and mismatched socks,
I navigate through paradoxical blocks.
Look at the puddle—what a sight,
Is it wisdom or just plain fright?

So I hop with glee, and splash with charm,
Riding the waves of this strange alarm.
Embrace confusion, let it persist,
As I dance through shadows, with a twirl and a twist.

In the mist, truths tend to bend,
But I laugh aloud, around every bend.
For often the path is a riddle and jest,
And the best part of me is a curious quest.

Chronicles of the Unknown

In the realm where questions roam free,
I've lost my socks, where could they be?
This quest for truth is a funny affair,
With giant rubber ducks floating in air.

Writing chapters on napkin delight,
With doodles of cats that take flight.
The unknown looms, like a sock-stealing ghost,
But I chuckle, because it's the fun I love most.

In the land of uncharted surprise,
Frogs wear crowns, and the sun is a prize.
So grab a friend, let's dance through the void,
With each silly moment, we're truthfully buoyed.

So here's to the tales we ponder and spin,
In a universe wobbly, let the joy begin.
With every chuckle, we sketch our own way,
At the end of the tale, we'll shout, "Hip hooray!"

The Breath of Expectations

I woke up this morning, feeling quite fine,
But my sock drawer had different plans, oh how it did whine!
Each foot a rebel, each step a strange dance,
I question my choices, but then take a chance.

The toast popped up, like a jack-in-the-box,
Burned on one side, its smell—like old socks.
I laughed at the chaos, poured coffee in haste,
Maybe today's magic is found in the waste.

An email arrives, another great deal,
A weight loss program, try the new meal!
I clicked on the link, now I'm lost in a maze,
I thought I was hungry, but I'm stuck in a daze.

Yet somewhere beneath this humorous spree,
I reckon I'll find what is truly for me.
With a sock and a slice of burnt toast on the side,
Here's to the laughter, let uncertainty slide.

Footprints in the Clouds

I looked up today, saw pigs flying by,
Thought of my dreams, like clouds in the sky.
Each one a concept, floaty and vague,
I grabbed my umbrella—oh, what a legague!

I chased them around till they scattered away,
Like a puppy at play, grabbing clouds on the sway.
What a pursuit, to catch joy on the run,
I fell on my back, laughing hard in the sun.

The footprints I leave are like breadcrumbs, you see,
Pointing to questions that go "who is me?"
Between each giggle, I ponder and muse,
Footprints in clouds, just whimsical views.

Yet here's a thought that brightens my plight:
If life were a joke, I'd need a good write!
So I'll cherish the laughter, with all I possess,
Perhaps understanding lies under this mess.

A Web of Contemplation

In the corner of my mind, a web starts to spin,
With thoughts tangled like spaghetti and a stray cat's grin.

I wonder if spiders know something I don't,
Or if they're just busy, totally at fault!

The more that I ponder, the more threads I weave,
Like I'm knitting a sweater no one would believe.
A scarf for the winter of doubt and despair,
Though it tickles my neck, I can't seem to care.

Each notion a fly, caught up in the glue,
I'm not so sure what I'm trying to do.
Maybe it's cozy, this odd little mess,
In a world full of chaos, I must confess.

So here's to the web, with hugs and with frowns,
I'll dance in its fibers and wear silly crowns.
With laughter, I'll unwind each silken strand,
Expectations still pending, but I'll make a stand.

Fragments of Tomorrow

I woke up with dreams, all scattered and wild,
Like toys on my floor, I'm still a lost child.
Those fragments of hope, they dance in my head,
Much like my breakfast, which quickly fled!

It's hard to assemble what seems quite absurd,
Like piecing a puzzle with one missing bird.
I'll grab all the colors, I'll paint them anew,
With splashes of laughter, this world feels askew.

The planner I bought, with its pages pristine,
Shows all my ambitions, though I'm stuck in between.
I scribble "next week," but tomorrow's a game,
I'm chasing my thoughts like a wild paper plane.

Yet maybe it's fine, this chaos and charm,
The fragments of moments might just bring me calm.
So I giggle and dance, let uncertainty be,
For tomorrow's just now, and I'm somehow free.

In Pursuit of Clarity

I sought the truth with fervent glee,
But it hid from me like a pesky flea.
The riddles danced, in jest they pranced,
Left me wondering what chance enhanced.

Grabbed a map with squiggly lines,
Thought I'd find where wisdom shines.
But every turn was a game of charades,
With a whisper of doubt in every cascade.

Grapes of knowledge looked sweet and ripe,
But tasted more like a sour type.
As I chuckled and scratched my head,
I tripped on questions that danced instead.

So here I stand, a fool with flair,
Chasing thoughts in the wild air.
In this jumble, confusion reigns,
Yet laughter blooms where nonsense gains.

The Road Not Yet Taken

I came across two paths today,
One looked dull, the other, yay!
I flipped a coin, and oh, how it spun,
Landed on 'leisure'—well, that's just fun!

The grass was greener on the detour lane,
Where squirrels held court; no one was sane.
I asked for directions from a wise old crow,
He cawed back, 'Just follow your woe!'

With every step, I laughed with delight,
Tripping on thoughts that danced in the night.
Should I follow plans or just take a leap?
In the end, it's all a giggle-fueled sweep.

So here I wander, lost yet free,
With a compass made of absurdity.
I'll take what comes with a wink and a grin,
After all, it's the chase that matters within.

Flickering Embers of Thought

In the fireplace of my mind,
Ideas flicker, never aligned.
Some are glowing, some just a spark,
But all of them dance in the dark.

I roast my questions like marshmallows sweet,
Giggling at answers that taste like defeat.
But the laughter keeps burning so bright,
While I ponder the oddities of night.

A jester's cap sits on my head,
As I juggle ideas like they're made of thread.
Why take it too seriously? What's the fuss?
When wisdom's a joke, and magic's a bus!

So I stir the embers, with a chuckle and cheer,
For amidst the chaos, clarity may near.
In a world where thoughts freely waltz,
I find joy in the muddle—turns out it's my pulse.

Navigating the Void

I set sail on the ocean of doubt,
With a map that seems to twist about.
My compass spins, what a messy show,
But the laughs just keep on like a wild rodeo!

Stars above wink with a cheeky grin,
As I drift on waves of whims within.
Each thought a fish, slippery and bright,
I catch them all—then they take flight!

What's the meaning of this grand parade?
Is it a dream or a cosmic charade?
I'll grab my oars and row with cheer,
In this void of nonsense, there's no need to fear.

So let's toast to the spaces between,
Where meaning emerges from the silly unseen.
With giggles and whispers, we'll navigate through,
The horizon of questions will greet me and you.

The Pause Before Dawn

In the stillness of the night,
Dreams dance like fireflies,
With thoughts of breakfast lurking,
And snores that shake the skies.

The coffee pot cries loudly,
While the cat has other plans,
Chasing shadows on the wall,
In a world of tiny scams.

The clock ticks, time's a joker,
Winking at us with delight,
Every minute like a riddle,
Wrapped in the softest light.

As dawn teases with its glow,
We stumble out of bed,
Chasing meaning in each moment,
Or just a bit of bread.

Color of the Unwritten

Blank pages stretch before me,
Like a vast and empty field,
Colors splashed in hesitation,
Awaiting brushstrokes revealed.

I dip my pen in nonsense,
Jokes and puns collide like hues,
Each line becomes a canvas,
For bizarre and playful views.

A sonnet turned to limerick,
With giggles in every meter,
Words dance like they're on vacation,
As wit tries to be the leader.

Unwritten thoughts give me wiggles,
As I ponder what I seek,
Perhaps it's all just nonsense,
Wrapped in giggles, not so bleak.

Sketches of a Dreamer

With crayons in a dreamer's hand,
I doodle out my plans,
A unicorn in patterned socks,
Dancing in the sand.

Each sketch brings forth a giggle,
As I erase with glee,
A dragon wearing flip-flops,
Oh, what could this all be?

In the margins of my notebook,
Life's questions tease and play,
While a hamster on a scooter
Takes my worries far away.

Sketches of thoughts lingering,
With colors splashed so bright,
Perhaps the art of dreaming
Is what makes every day light.

Mysteries of the Heart

Love notes scribbled on napkins,
With doodles that make me smile,
Finding joy in endless puzzles,
That stretch over many a mile.

A kiss like a flying donut,
Sweet and always out of reach,
While the heart rolls like a tumbleweed,
In a game of hide-and-seek.

Riddles wrapped in laughter,
Giggles hiding in my chest,
What is this thing called affection?
Wings that never seem to rest.

In the chaos of emotions,
I dance without a care,
For the mysteries that tease my soul,
Are simply giggles in the air.

Mapping the Infinite Now

I bought a map of nowhere,
Filled it with big red X's.
Each turn I take gets me lost,
Yet still I ask for directions.

The GPS says to go straight,
But Starbucks is just ahead.
I take a right, ignore the fate,
And end up in a donut bed.

My compass spins like a top,
Every point seems just as true.
I'm here, I'm there, and then I stop,
To wonder, who's fooling who?

With every step, I trip and fall,
On my own feet, such a clown.
Mapping chaos, having a ball,
In this here infinite town.

The Stillness Between Dreams

In dreamland, I float on clouds,
Where unicorns wear silly hats.
They dance and sing of nothing loud,
While I'm perplexed by my own chats.

Awake, I find the fridge is bare,
Yet in my dreams, I feast like kings.
I swear the snooze button's not fair,
While my bed softly pulls on strings.

Between the pillows, wisdom hides,
Telling me to sleep a bit more.
But I stumble out like a deer,
Tripping over a laundry floor.

With coffee in hand and a yawn,
I wonder what the dreams would bring.
But I just want one more dawn,
To dance with my sheets in spring.

Chords of an Unstruck Heart

My heart plays music, so they say,
But it keeps missing all the notes.
I'm dancing on a sunny ray,
While croaking like a bunch of goats.

Trying to strum a gentle tune,
But a cat jumps on the keys.
I laugh and sing beneath the moon,
This symphony's full of trees.

The violins are out of tune,
As I tap dance on the floor.
The kazoo sounds like a raccoon,
And yet, who could ask for more?

So here we jam, amidst the chaos,
With every chord a new surprise.
My unstruck heart sings in pathos,
Creating laughter in the skies.

A Dance on the Edge of Tomorrow

Tomorrow wears mismatched socks,
As I step into the fray.
I trip on yesterday's old rocks,
While dancing in a clumsy way.

With coffee cups as my ballet,
I swirl and twirl around the room.
Stumbling like I've gone astray,
Creating a spectacular gloom.

The clock ticks loudly, mocking me,
Yet I embrace the silly hour.
This dance is pure absurdity,
With laughter as my finest power.

So here's to moves I can't define,
As I twirl into the next refrain.
Life's a stage, wobbly, divine,
And tomorrow's dance will drive me insane!

Pathways of Wonder

I wandered down the garden path,
Where daisies smiled and squirrels laughed.
But what is this? A snail on cue,
Wearing a hat, quite dapper too!

With butterflies dancing all around,
I pondered why time is always bound.
It tickles my toes, a riddle it tells,
While bees buzz loud like playful bells.

Oh, what if socks had secret dreams?
And coffee spilled out sunlit beams?
We'd toast with muffins, joyfully bright,
With toast in hand, we'd giggle all night!

In puddles deep, I jump and splash,
Why do grown-ups hurry, going in a flash?
Perhaps in clouds, the answers play,
On pathways of wonder, I'll drift away!

The Space Between Questions

What if my shoes had something to say?
Would they whisper secrets of yesterday?
Each squeak and squish, a tale they spin,
Of puddles danced and places we've been.

The clock on the wall just winks at me,
Saying, "Chill out! Just wait and see!"
With a tick-tock laugh, it pauses to tease,
"Why race with time when you could just sneeze?"

In conversations with cats, oh what a sight,
They plot and they plan in the pale moonlight.
I live in a world where odd things blend,
Maybe the question's the answer, my friend!

So let's sip our tea and float like a balloon,
Discussing the weather and singing to the moon.
In the space between questions, we find our song,
In the curious pauses, where we belong!

Silent Conversations

Underneath the stars, I chat with the night,
While crickets provide the music to my flight.
With hiccuping owls in amusing debates,
I ponder why food is sometimes on plates!

A wink from the moon, a whisper so soft,
As shadows hold secrets of laughter aloft.
What if my dreams wear pajamas too?
Draped in stardust, a periwinkle hue!

I asked a pen why it wrote my fate,
It scribbled back, "Oh, that's up for debate!"
Then rolled away, feeling quite bold,
It seems ink also likes to be told!

So here we are, in this nonsensical chat,
With laughter that dances like a fancy hat.
In silent conversations, we draw the line,
Finding humor hidden, oh how divine!

Chasing Shadows

In a park filled with laughter, we chase shadows bright,
I trip on a giggle, oh what a sight!
Umbrellas do jiggles to the rhythm of trees,
And squirrels hold conferences with all of the bees.

What if my thoughts were bubbles like these?
Floating away on the lightest breeze?
Each idea a flavor, sweet and sour too,
In this circus of nonsense, I share them with you!

A sandwich once told me it wanted to fly,
So we packed it a picnic and waved it goodbye.
With mustard and joy, it soared through the sky,
Chasing sunbeams, the world passing by.

As dusk paints the scene, we laugh at the day,
In a world so absurd, we shout, "Hooray!"
With shadows in tow, we skip on the way,
Finding fun in the moments, come what may!

Spaces Yet to Fill

In a world of whims, we jog,
Chasing dreams like a three-legged dog.
With pockets of hopes and a cap full of fears,
We dance, we fall, we bump into mirrors.

Life's a jigsaw, pieces tossed high,
Search for the edge pieces, oh my, oh my!
With laughter we glide, we skip and we twirl,
Even when chaos makes our heads whirl.

Each door is a riddle, each sign is a clue,
We throw paper planes to see what is true.
The sky's full of questions, the ground needs a joke,
In this puzzling game, we're all just a bloke.

So let's sip our coffee and ponder the thrill,
While we search for the reason behind the free will.
With a pinch of absurdity, a dash of delight,
We'll embrace the absurdity, day into night.

The Heart's Inquiry

The heart is a lawyer with cases to plead,
Arguing daily about wants and need.
It files all the feelings like bills in a stack,
Trying to figure out what it all lacks.

There's love in the fridge, but it's expired,
Yet we cling to the hope—how inspired!
With chocolate and laughter, the jury convicts,
If joy is the gavel, let's work our tricks.

Questions like ants march around in our heads,
Biting our thoughts like soft, buttery breads.
The heart rolls its eyes, taps its little toes,
While the body just wonders how much longer it goes.

So here's to the queries that tickle our minds,
To awkward decisions and comical finds.
With every new heartbeat, we scribble down notes,
As the funny old heart keeps spinning its quotes.

Beyond What We Know

To galaxies far with bizarre little things,
We squint through the glass as the universe sings.
What's out there, we wonder, in this cosmic ballet?
Maybe just cows having tea by the bay.

Perhaps there's a planet made wholly of cheese,
Where socks are the currency and time's just a breeze.
With penguins as leaders and cats that do math,
We dream about journeys embarked on a path.

In every new blink, theories twist and collide,
As we sail through the stars on a comet's fun ride.
So pass me a snack, let's debate on the way,
If outside's a circus, we'll laugh while we play.

The mysteries wait with a wink and a grin,
While we chase wild answers, let the adventure begin!
'Cause beyond what we know is the chaos we crave,
And in this vast comedy, we're daring and brave.

Echoes Through Time

In the halls of the past, echoes bounce like a ball,
  Whispers of laughter, and oh! Did you recall?
The posters of worries tape our minds to the wall,
  While mishaps and giggles form a long, silly hall.

Tick-tock goes the clock, and we dance in a line,
  With each tick we stumble, a misstep divine.
Hindsight's a joker, with tricks up its sleeve,
  Like pinching a nose just to give it some heave.

We peek through the curtains of time with a grin,
  Seeking the moments where laughter begins.
With silver linings glittering from stories of old,
  We toast to the echoes, both silly and bold.

So let's scribble our tales on the fabric of fate,
  With joy we'll remember, it's never too late.
For in every tick-tock, there's a chuckle and cheer,
  While echoes through time are the essence we steer.

To the Edge of Knowing

I woke up today, what a surprise,
Thought I had answers, but what a disguise!
Coffee in hand, yet my mind's still a mess,
Chasing conclusions, oh what a jest!

Google was helpful, or so I believed,
But now I'm just more confused than relieved.
Searching for wisdom in cat memes online,
Maybe enlightenment needs more than just wine!

Questions keep piling, a curious stack,
Like socks missing their partners, it's quite the attack.
Each thought leads to ten, a veritable spree,
Am I learning or just a lost bumblebee?

So here I stand, on the edge of my seat,
With laughter to mask this absurd little feat.
The quest for the answers is hilariously grand,
And maybe, just maybe, I'll still understand!

Fragments of a Daydream

In the land of pancakes and flying cows,
I searched for meaning, but forgot my vows.
Sipping on syrup, I pondered my fate,
While my cat plotted how to navigate!

Thoughts drift like butter on a warm piece of toast,
Is pondering an art, or just a good boast?
Some say the answers are hid in plain sight,
But I think they're lost in the fridge, out of spite!

I scribble my questions on napkins and dreams,
With doodles of llamas and bright, silly beams.
In fragments I find my grand little quest,
And wonder if napping might just be the best!

A daydream's a puzzle, with pieces all blurred,
I grab a snack, and my thoughts get deferred.
Maybe the truth is to laugh and to sing,
And let the absurdity dance on a swing!

Uncharted Territories

Today I embarked on a journey quite grand,
With my trusty old map made of pocket lint and sand.
Venturing forth into places unknown,
Mapped only by snacks and a slightly loud groan!

With every step, my thoughts do collide,
Like socks in the dryer, they swirl and they slide.
Is that wisdom I smell, or just yesterday's fries?
Searching for treasure, or perhaps just some pies?

Exploring the nooks of my cluttered brain,
Dodging the thoughts that just drive me insane.
This uncharted land, full of giggles and shouts,
Might lead to some truths, or just rowdy doubts!

So off I will march, with my compass askew,
In search of the answers, that may not be true.
As long as I laugh and enjoy what I find,
These adventures of folly are the best for the mind!

A Canvas of Questions

With brushes and colors, I paint on my mind,
A canvas of questions, each one unconfined.
Dabbing on worries, mixing up fears,
Creating a masterpiece from laughter and tears!

Why is chocolate better than broccoli greens?
Is happiness found in the sound of machines?
The palette is crowded, with ideas in flux,
Paint spills like laughter, oh what a deluxe!

I splatter my thoughts like confetti in air,
And giggle at wonders that whisper, "Who cares?"
With every stroke, a new question appears,
Maybe the answers just taste better with cheers!

So here's to the canvas, a messy delight,
Where pondering life's quirks brings giggles at night.
In this carnival of doubts and bright hues,
I'll laugh at the absurd, and sing my own blues!

Underneath the Surface

Beneath the waves, a fish did plea,
"What's the point? Just let me be!"
He swam in circles, round and round,
While jellyfish danced without a sound.

A crab with glasses tried to think,
"Is there more than just this drink?"
He sipped his seaweed, lost in thought,
While bubbles rose, and wisdom fought.

A dolphin joked, "What's the deal?"
"We flip and flop, but what's the reel?"
The ocean shrugged, said, "Just float!"
Too deep for questions like a goat.

So here we are, just swimming through,
While clownfish giggle, and the seaweed grew.
With every wave, a joke unfurled,
Beneath the surface of a silly world.

Journeys Yet to Embark

A snail packed bags, all ready to go,
"I'll find the answers, don't you know?"
He slipped on shoes, one foot at a time,
Until he tripped, and fell in grime.

A frog on a lily took a big leap,
"To search for purpose, not just a sheep!"
But missed the pad and fell with a splat,
"Oh, what a journey! How about that?"

A turtle slumped and scratched his shell,
"Maybe the quest is just to dwell?"
While ants marched by in lines so neat,
"We're on our way—where's the cheat sheet?"

So dreams of travel may bring some cheer,
But sometimes the couch is the best frontier.
With snacks in hand, we'll plot and plan,
For journeys we'll take, if only we can.

Shadows of Purpose

In the park, a shadow danced,
It tripped on grass, and then it pranced.
"What's the goal?" it seemed to ask,
"I'm just a shade, it's quite a task!"

A cat in sun slipped into pose,
"Is chasing mice the end? Who knows!"
With every pounce, a blur of fur,
"I may not catch, but I'll confer!"

The wind sighed softly, with a laugh,
"I'm just a breeze, I'm not your path!"
It tugged at leaves, and danced away,
"Stop asking me, live day by day!"

So shadows come and shadows go,
In search of purpose, neat or low.
We trip and tumble, trip some more,
In silly questions, we'll not ignore.

When Stars Still Wonder

When stars were born, they danced in fright,
"Will we shine bright, or lose our light?"
They twirled in space, all shimmering,
Yet questions swirled, and none were king.

A comet zoomed with a wobbly tail,
"Is chasing dreams worth the hail?"
It zipped through skies, in spirals steep,
While lingering doubts made starlight weep!

Galaxies chuckled, a vast, loud roar,
"We're just here for the cosmic floor!"
In endless spin, they spun away,
While holding hands, they chose to play.

So when you look up, see stars in wonder,
Remember their journey through thunder and blunder.
It's not just light, but laughter too,
In this cosmic dance, we're all in view.

Dreams in Transition

In dreams I chase a dancing cat,
It wears a hat, a tale to spat.
Through doors that lead to nowhere fast,
I wonder where my dreams are cast.

I trip on thoughts that jump around,
In silly socks, I'm homeward bound.
With ice cream towers reaching high,
I question if I can just fly.

The clock strikes twelve, it's time for tea,
With talking fish, they're friends of me.
We sip on whims and share our fluff,
And ponder if that's quite enough.

But as the sun begins to rise,
Those cat and fish, they wave goodbye.
I'm back to work, yet doubt remains,
Will dreams come back with all their gains?

Beyond the Familiar

I stepped outside my comfy crib,
And found a place where chickens fib.
They clucked advice on stocks and bonds,
While roaming cats played silly songs.

A giraffe wrote poems in the park,
And squirrels danced till after dark.
I tripped upon a lost shoe's fate,
Where every step would make me late.

The sun wore shades, a cool charade,
As time tick-tocked, I was betrayed.
I laughed at clouds with grumpy glares,
And high-fived trees who claimed their chairs.

But inside me, there's still a quest,
For answers hiding, fully dressed.
I'll tip my hat and take the leap,
Tomorrow's fun, who knows, or keep?

The Unfinished Tale

Once upon a time, or was it twice?
A dragon sneezed and rolled some dice.
He conjured dreams from cheesy pies,
While knights played tag in fuzzy ties.

A princess in a paper crown,
Declared that laughter was the town.
But scribbles filled the pages left,
A plot so loose, it felt quite bereft.

With magic beans stuck in a joke,
The fairy godmother cracked, then spoke.
'To finish this, let's spice it right,
Add flying pigs to the moonlight!'

So here we are, in this grand stew,
A tale still brewing, yet it's true.
With every laugh, we weave and wail,
Our story's dance, a twisted trail.

Spaces in Between

In the gaps between socks and sweat,
I find my dreams, a little pet.
A sock drawer hides a bustling street,
Where mismatched thoughts and laughter meet.

Under beds, my worries play,
They tiptoe out, and then they sway.
A dust bunny waves, it spins around,
With secret tales that know no bound.

The curtains flap, they whisper low,
Of half-formed hopes and treasures stowed.
I dance with shadows, twirl and glide,
In these strange spaces, I confide.

So here's to gaps and middle grounds,
Where lost ideas become the sounds.
I will embrace what's still to be,
In this great space, just wait and see.

The Search for Essence

In a room full of socks, I ponder and muse,
What's the purpose of pizza? And do I want good views?
Questions dance like shadows, a wild little troupe,
Trying to find the meaning, while I'm stuck with a stoop.

Coffee spills like secrets, hot and sometimes bitter,
I seek wisdom in crumbs, and I bet my cat's the sitter.
Is there joy in the static, the mundane and the bland?
Or is it just a setup for a quirky band?

What if happiness hides in my sock drawer's embrace?
Or maybe in that old guide, 'How to win at a race'?
Jokes scribbled on napkins, with ketchup stains bright,
Whisper sweet nothings, in the chaos of night.

I chase after shadows, they giggle and run,
Where's my pot of gold? Is it all just for fun?
In the dance of confusion, I'll waltz with a grin,
For the search is the essence, where the humor begins.

Questions in the Quiet

Why is a toaster so reliable on bread?
But never once whispers on thoughts in my head?
I ponder while sipping my drink, so divine,
Is the meaning of life found in cookies and wine?

Ducks waddle by silently judging my stance,
They quack with conviction, as if they had plans.
I ask them for answers, but they just float away,
Chasing clouds instead of the lessons to stay.

Amongst the socks and the dust bunnies' flight,
I scribble my worries in dim candlelight.
With laughter in echoes, I glean bits of gold,
The quiet holds secrets the bold haven't told.

A plant in the corner sways back with a sigh,
Does it know why we're here? Or just wondering why?
Should I trust my heart or that strange little sock?
Perhaps, like a clock, I just tick and I mock.

Echoes of a Dream

In dreams, I am dancing with socks on my feet,
Giggling with shadows, oh life's such a treat!
I ride on a llama through fields of bright cheese,
Is this what they meant by the art of appease?

With tangerines talking and clouds wearing hats,
I roam through the meadows with playful good bats.
Do dreams hold the answers, or merely just fluff?
I awaken and wonder, is that really enough?

Floating through nonsense, I chase after glee,
The laughter of whimsy, should it bother me?
I pick up relationships like odd pairs of socks,
And muse over quirks of those wise little rocks.

Echoes of nonsense fill rooms with delight,
In the twilight of pondering, I twirl in the night.
For maybe the essence is hidden in cheer,
With a wink and a giggle, we'll figure it here!

Between the Lines of Existence

In the margins of life, between giggles and sighs,
Lies a riddle of sorts that tickles the skies.
What if tomorrow just borrowed today's plans?
With a wink from a potato and hug from the cans?

Stumbling on answers like tripping on dreams,
I scribble my thoughts in whimsical streams.
Is the meaning in balance, or is it in fun?
Should I chase down the sunset or run with a bun?

A pickle and onion both ponder and grin,
Do they have insights that I'll never win?
Or are they just sauces that laughter can bring?
In a sandwich of wisdom, I feast on the swing.

So let's paint our questions with splashes of joy,
With a twist and a shout, like a cheeky young boy.
Maybe the truths hide in the laughter we share,
Between silly moments, we find what is rare.

Charting the Unseen

In a world full of signs, we seek the clues,
But end up with puzzles and lots of blues.
Maps in our minds with paths gone astray,
We scribble and giggle, it's just our way.

Searching for wisdom in a cereal box,
Finding deep truths in the strangest of talks.
With each little question, we dance and we prance,
Clueless yet cheerful, we give it a chance.

With theories and whispers, we gather the crew,
To decipher the meanings of "maybe" and "who?"
We toast to confusion with laughter and cheer,
Cuz searching for answers just brings us near.

So let's chart the unseen, let laughter be our guide,
In this unpredictable, top-secret ride.
We might never know, but we'll shrug and proceed,
With a wink and a wiggle, we embrace the need.

The Inbetween of Knowing

In the middle of yes and a casual maybe,
We twirl like lost socks, feeling quite crazy.
Questions pop up like daisies in spring,
"Why are we here?" Oh, what joy to bring!

We flip through the pages of fate's funny book,
Hoping for glimmers when we take a look.
The riddles of breakfast, the mysteries of tea,
What makes toast golden? Who knows? Not me!

In the dance of the doubt, we all join the waltz,
Trying to figure out whose fault's whose faults.
With giggles and shrugs, we toss logic aside,
In the inbetween, our laughter's our guide.

So here we sit, on this whimsical ride,
Chasing the shadows where secrets reside.
With a chuckle and grin, we jump in the fray,
Embracing the chaos, come what may!

Voices of the Untold

In the murmur of whispers, the voices collide,
Tales of the silly in shadows they hide.
A chicken crossed roads, without much ado,
To find out what makes the grass greener too!

Echoes of laughter bound tightly in air,
While fish tell their stories of swimming with flair.
The llama and owl, in a riddle contest,
Ask who's the wisest? They both say, "We jest!"

Unfolding the narratives woven in rhyme,
We giggle at clarities lost in the grime.
Every untold secret finds comedic release,
Wrapping absurdity in bundles of peace.

Let's listen in closely, to the chatter around,
For wisdom is silly, in echoes we've found.
In the chorus of nonsense, we find strength and gold,
As we uncover the laughter in stories untold.

Explorations in Ambivalence

In the land of 'quite' and 'maybe' we lounge,
Dodging decisions like they're a strange clown.
Do we stay or go? Flip a coin, have a snack,
Each option we ponder sends logic off track.

We're masters of fence-sitting, lounge-chair kings,
Debating where hope and absurdity clings.
In this maelstrom of choices, we giggle and scoff,
Stuck in our paradox, but we still take a cough.

From pizza to salad, we dance with the doubt,
Should we jump on the train or just hang out?
Our minds play on loops, a fantastic charade,
As we juggle our whims amid humor displayed.

So here's to the muddle, the chaos so bright,
In each twist and turn of the day and the night.
With laughs as our compass, let's embrace the wild,
In explorations of ambivalence, we're all just a child.

Threads of Hope

In a world where socks disappear,
I search for purpose year by year.
With mismatched dreams and coffee stains,
I ponder if it all remains.

A fridge full of old takeout bliss,
I wonder what I truly miss.
Between the bites and silly jokes,
I find a truth among the pokes.

Dance of chaos, run amok,
Clumsy strides, we're out of luck.
Yet giggles sprout like daisies bright,
Through every stumble, joy takes flight.

With threads of hope, I'll weave my tale,
A patchwork life as winds prevail.
Unsure where it'll lead me next,
But hey, at least I'm often vexed!

Beyond the Horizon

I sailed away from common shores,
To find what waits, behind closed doors.
With waves of questions, sails of doubt,
I shouted, 'What's this all about?'

Around me, gulls fly high and free,
While I'm just lost—where could I be?
An ocean vast, my thoughts a mess,
I make a joke, yes, I confess.

Beyond the horizon, what's out there?
Possibly snacks or a millionaire?
With each new wave, I laugh and cheer,
Adventures loom, but so does fear!

So here I float, on dreams I cast,
With a surfboard made of memories past.
And when I find that distant land,
I'll start again, with snacks on hand!

Tides of Uncertainty

The tide rolls in, and so do doubts,
With questions swirling all about.
Do I eat cake, or hit the gym?
My choices here are looking grim!

Each wave that crashes brings a thought,
Is finding joy so easily bought?
While rubber ducks float here and there,
I wonder if they have a care.

The moon pulls me, its glow so bright,
Yet here I am, a silly sight.
I'll ride these tides with laughter loud,
In wobbly boats, we're all quite proud!

So here I splash in shallow streams,
Where every ripple fuels my dreams.
With each uncertain, bumpy ride,
I'll take a seat and enjoy the glide!

The Dance of Possibilities

In a giddy whirl, I leap and twirl,
With quirky moves, I make you hurl.
The dance of what could be tonight,
With two left feet, oh what a sight!

I spin on thoughts that twist and shout,
And trip over dreams that flit about.
While moonlight giggles, stars all cheer,
I wobble on—'Is this sincere?'

With every step and stuttered beat,
I find a rhythm, can't be beat.
In this grand ball of fate's design,
I laugh at fate, so divine!

So join this dance and feel the sway,
As life's absurdity leads the way.
With every misstep, joy expands,
In this wacky world, let's take our stands!

Curious Echoes

In the halls of thought, I wander,
Where answers giggle, just beyond my grasp.
Every question's like a cheeky fonder,
Hiding from me, like a contorted rasp.

My mind's a circus, laughter rings,
Juggling doubts like a silly clown.
Wondering if I'll find the wings,
To soar past wonders, upside down.

Each echo calls with a playful jest,
A riddle wrapped in a sock of dreams.
Should I chase or just let rest?
Even my thoughts disagree, it seems.

Yet in this dance of bizarre delight,
I trip through truths with a snort and a grin.
Perhaps the joy's in the silly fight,
And the punchline waits, just skin-deep within.

The Weight of Untold Stories

My tales are stacked like a lopsided chair,
Each wobble tells of things left unsaid.
With every wiggle, I feel the weight there,
As if my secrets weigh down my head.

In coffee shops, my thoughts arise,
Like balloons tied to a stubborn chair.
Floating high, we wave goodbyes,
To seriousness, beyond compare.

The plot thickens like a stew on the fire,
I spill it all, but it just won't cook.
A spoonful of truth and a dash of liar,
What was that story? I lost the hook.

So here I sit, a storyteller meek,
Tripping on words with a grin so wide.
Perhaps the punchline's what we seek,
In the laughter of tales that can't abide.

Grains of Uncertainty

Like grains of sand, my thoughts shift and sway,
Filling the hourglass with paths untried.
Questions tumble in a zany array,
Where logic's dance doesn't abide.

Each grain a dream, too fragile to hold,
Bouncing around like a pinball machine.
Are there answers? Or stories untold?
The more I ponder, the less I glean.

I build castles, but they fall with a laugh,
As waves of confusion wash them all away.
In this grand game, I'm a comical staff,
With script still being written, day by day.

Yet through the mess, a chuckle does leak,
At the silliness of seeking a sign.
Life's like a riddle that loves to sneak,
Leaving us giggling, lost in the line.

Threads of a Cosmic Tapestry

In the loom of stars, I weave my thread,
A tapestry of giggles, twinkling bright.
Each knot a question that dances ahead,
Chasing its tail into the night.

Is there a pattern, or simply a mess?
A cosmic quilt that charms with each fold.
Finding answers feels more like a jest,
Like socks mismatched, yet still being sold.

I pull at fibers, inspecting each hue,
Wondering why there's no easy seam.
Do they hold secrets, or just view a view,
Of a universe wrapped in its own dream?

So I stitch with chuckles, and humor's delight,
Embracing the chaos of cosmic design.
Perhaps in this whimsy, we'll find that bright,
Thread of connection, or just some good wine.

www.ingramcontent.com/pod-product-compliance
Lightning Source LLC
Chambersburg PA
CBHW071834160426
43209CB00003B/294